LATE DAYS

Michael Glover &
Ruth Dupré

www.1889books.co.uk

For our friends Peter and Madeleine Elliott, in whose house near Carcassonne *Late Days* was written

ISBN 978-0-9935762-8-7

www.1889books.co.uk

in memory of Aunt Honor Dupré

You see, I am writing all this at odd moments, and in different ways, as the mood strikes, as the memories of my life wash in and out. Some parts of it are like a story that I am telling myself, that I really *want* to tell myself in order to give myself pleasure, and perhaps in order to distract me from being here. Other parts, not so easy to describe or to categorise, are more like poems, and that is why I have made them *look* like poems, breaking them up into short lines, ranging them down the page, so that you will read them more slowly. Some of those pieces even I puzzle over, so I would not be at all surprised if you found yourself puzzling over them too.

And none of this is at all finished because it is tumbling out, bit by bit, as the days go by, in no particular order, and I want it to be like that because I want you to feel it as I felt it, and to read it as I wrote it, as if it were a record of my own breathing, moment by moment, because that will tell you more about me than would be the case if someone were to take it apart and try to organise it more tidily, pretending that it was a novel or a story with a tidy beginning, middle and end.

It is as if I am a child again, standing on a Cornish cliff, looking at the sea, which seems to be changing colour all the time, ever restless. Part of me is trying to make sense of everything for your sake, you see, to explain it all to you, to present it to you, as if it could be put in a box like a gift. But it is not really like that. It is more like a jigsaw puzzle, with a thousand pieces, all so awkwardly shaped. I don't quite know how it all fits together because there are always so many parts to it, and some of them suit one way of telling while others are so ungovernable I scarcely know what to do with them, so I bundle them off into poem-shapes and hope for the best, and I hope you will forgive me for that because I now think I understand that people often do not always grasp hold of the meaning of the whole of their own lives. It is always so surprising what comes, sometimes unbidden – a particular look on Freddy's face when he was very, very tiny and not really angry about anything at all as far as I could see, or Maggie stomping around, making the bedroom floor shudder in her big, stompy shoes, and my saying to her, quite crossly: ssssssh! (I should tell you, of course, that I have always loved jigsaw puzzles, the greater the number of pieces the better. I do one every day, leaving it half-finished on a tray, so that when one or other of my niece's children comes down to tea, they can join in and help me.)

My Father's Voice

There must be some advantages to living here, with all this lovely morning light streaming in through the window... (My father's voice again, one doodle-bug-free morning in Battersea. Would this war never end?) *Take this desk, for example, and how in time, child of mine, you will accustom yourself to sitting at it...*

Father's knuckles, rap-rapping on the desk top.
And rap-rapping at my skull too,
though gently enough
because he was never a fierce man
even when, head sunk low on his chest,
his hand clutched at a letter,
which he would then carefully fold away
into his pocket...

My Mother's Voice

The night winds always blow too fiercely for you!
Were those her first words to me?
Or has my remembering gone astray again?
She was grazing my cheek with her finger.
I had hidden my head beneath the eiderdown
until my cheeks began to sweat.

I had made a nest for myself,
and when she came calling, much later,
the sound of her voice blew in like a wind
from some place faraway.

Mother! Mother! I was saying back to her,
but in a voice so indistinct that I knew she could not
possibly hear me. My breathing voice
came so strong in my ears.

Mother, mother, do hear me now.
I am saying it again. I am saying it out loud.
Why are you not here with me today?
Instead, there is a hollow bowl,
Set down here on my bedside table
Expressly to catch the sputum,
A bowl which shines today as bright
As that suit of armour in the Wallace Collection
To which we were all being taken because today
Is a cultural London Sunday.

Every second Sunday, let me remind you,
father says to me, as I go to open my cupboard
with all its special things
after a hearty breakfast of two fried eggs
and a single rasher of bacon,
is a cultural London Sunday.

I am poking about.
I am trying to find my warm mittens.
Do not let yourself be distracted,
he adds, hands across my shoulders,
from the important things of life, Daisy, my lady.

On the crest of the hill,
from where we could see and see
Almost as far as Hampstead Heath,
We would lie on our sides,
roll ourselves up like a ball
and let ourselves go
to the accompaniment of squeals of pleasure.

And father would run beside us as we rolled,
shouting encouragement, and even giving us a gentle
push with his toe.
By way of encouragement, you must understand.
You see, that was the man that he was
and would always be. Until he wasn't.

My father is taller than a telegraph pole.
I would point and point, laughing,
As he rose up on the tips of his toes
To prove that everything I said was true,
In fact just as true as the day,
this day's sky, is a clear blue.

Parallel Dyings

Did he die before I died? It is all so unclear to me.
Or is he not dying now,
just a little, inside me, as I too am dying?
Both of us now, in such camaraderie,
dying together, the older and the yet older still,
making this compact of sorts, to die together,
to prove how much we have loved
and do still love each other,

to prove that our lives are still running in parallel
like the trains that moved with such majesty
out of Paddington Station that morning –
was it a Tuesday? –
that morning we went West for our holiday treat,
that morning of my childhood
which I am cradling today in my arms,
not letting it go,
not letting it go forever.

You see, I am making this book for you all, for all my family gathered here around this bed – there is such a crowd of you here today! – so that you do not turn aside and too quickly forget me.

It is imperative that you do not forget me because I have been too much here, for far too long, to be readily forgotten. I have stamped my foot so fiercely on this earth, time and again, for you not to wish to go on noticing me – for a little while at least.

Maggie, are you there for me? Have you gone before then?
And, if so, are you still waiting?
Or are you distracted with all your nonsense this morning,
as you were always distracted,
much to my exasperation, because I believed, always,
in serious things, and you evidently did not.

The twin paths, the morning paths down the garden,
were always tinged with blue, and I was the only one to notice.
I would take a bowl and a spoon,
and very carefully, I would skim off the blueness –
it was always on the very top –
and carry it back to the kitchen,
where I would ask for it to be stirred and mixed
with a little self-raising flour and a little water,
and when the mixture had a certain thickness –
it never took long – I would drink it down to the dregs,
and make myself feel light of head.
Nothing ever troubled me about any of this.
I knew that I had partaken of
the pure goodness of the paths of our morning garden.

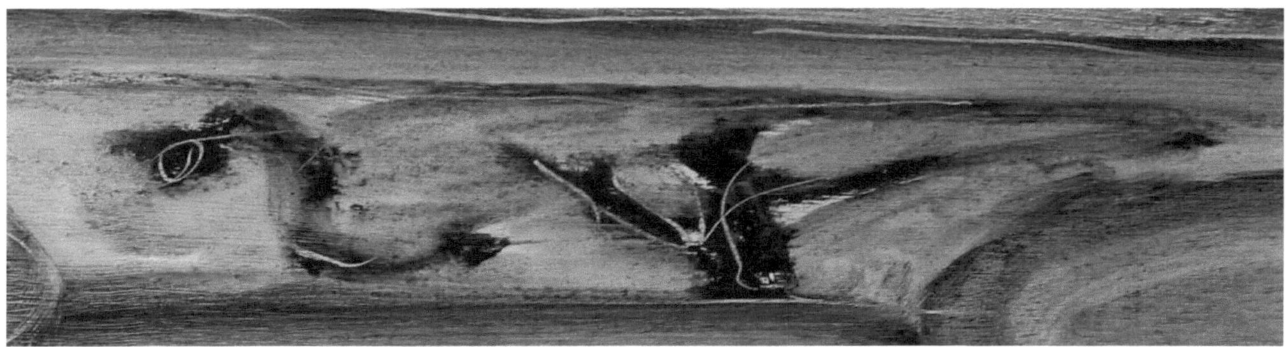

Suckling

I took you from our mother's arms, Frederick,
my precious, warm, sideways-on vase of a baby.
I cleanly lifted you aside.
And then I held you to my child's breast
and pretended to suckle you,
making the sounds you always made
when you took mother's milk

as I looked on, holding a glass of my own,
and even sipping at it as you sucked,
though mine was the milkman's gift,
that lovely, red-faced man
who always made the bottles jangle
when he lifted them from his cart
and then offered them,
two in each hand,
one to each of us.

I am a sad child today.
The letters are all facing the wrong way,
and all kindness has gone away.

I know that from the way
father raised his voice today
when he heard that stern voice,

carried on the radio's waves,
and then walked so hurriedly away
without even noticing me

or remembering my favourite name.

The Stairs

My bones feel much older than I think I am today.
Here are the stairs that I must climb again.
I place my hand on the banister rail.
They are my stairs.
I have lived inside them half my life
as a cold hand lives inside a winter glove.

And now, as I raise each leg,
I find myself protesting against them
for the pain they now cause me.
And yet they are not to blame.
It is my entire body which is to blame.
My body no longer does what it is required to do.

It asks me to wait a little longer.
It baulks at new challenges,
scarcely recognising that these are the old challenges.
It may be time to throw this body away.
I feel gratified that these stairs will remain.
I would not have them suffer for my shortcomings
as a faltering, fading human being.

Someone came close just then,
and did not touch me.
My eyes were closed when it happened.
I was only half attentive.

And yet someone came close,
and that someone – man, woman or child –
examined me with his eye
and then left again

without saying a single word to me.
They stole something from me
and they did not tell me.
They had some thought about me

and they did not share it.
Were I able,
I would jump out of this bed,
seize a stick from a corner,

and beat them within an inch of their lives
for such a display of impertinence.
Am I a thing to be gawped at
and then tossed aside?

You lifted me from one place to another
as carefully as you were able.
When the stretcher tilted up

as I was carried backwards up the ambulance's steps,
I felt the bones in my broken shoulder grind together.
But you were not to know.

You were not responsible.
You were looking on me kindly
when I clenched my teeth and closed my eyes.

The best part of all was mid-way through the journey,
when I saw the great river flowing beside me,
with such ease and such confidence.

It granted me my muttered wish just then:
Sweet Thames, my river of rivers, oh yes,
do buoy me and enfold me.

I am here at last,
and this does feel like the last of me.
I have spoken those words to you.
I have written my final letter.
Are there other matters for which I must be held accountable?
Surely there must be.

Family Portrait

The dog sat in front of us all,
making it difficult for us to settle.
It was too eager to be petted,
and we were too eager to be doing the petting.

And then you laughed when his head disappeared
beneath the black hood.
You called him a monster.
We all started to giggle.

Father had to be called back from his study
to give us a good telling off.
No one could smile for the camera after that
or worse would surely have happened.

What then is resignation?
Is it to say nothing?
Is it to be carried out to sea by the waves,
floating on one's back,
seeing nothing but the hurrying clouds,
and fearing nothing?
Yes, perhaps it is that.

I have a home to return to,
and I shall return to it a little later
when all this fuss and bother is over.
I have every confidence that it is all before me.

I have my childhood yet to live,
and all the coming days of my maturity.
It is merely a matter of lying here
and showing a little patience.

I must not let things get to me.
I have written all that down on a piece of paper
on this trolley beside me.

They wheel me somewhere.
And then they return me here.
I have no say in the matter.
My life is not my own any more.

What use is it all now?
I want it to go away.
It is all too wearisomely familiar,
everything that I have always been.

Give me the gift of endless sleep.
Give me the gift of not needing to ask for a thing.
They pry too much. They come too often.
I want them to take their leave of me.

And then we were all making such a din that no one could be heard, least of all father, who was mouthing some words above us all – I could see his mouth, his lips working. I could see how his face was reddening, as it so often did when he saw to the fire, jousting with the flames, horn-handled poker in hand. Father is not happy, I said, and I pointed up at him. At that, they all stopped what they were doing, and everyone, the whole uproariously noisy party, looked up, as if rather ashamed, and agreed as one to feel very, very sorry for him.

Father, you see, I am good for something.

I have a use for these bells, even when you tell me that they are not ringing, and that they are only ringing in my head. Are you unkind to say that to me? I regard myself as prayerfully attentive to the least little thing today, as if an entire layer of my life has been peeled away to reveal something astonishing underneath. I had no time for such thinking when I was a young girl. I was always running, so breathlessly running, to get somewhere, even when that somewhere was barely anywhere to speak of. Would you please stay for a little while so that I can explain all this to you, how I have matured, what has happened to me? All this is quite special to me, and I want you to know. It is all so recent! Why then, when I tell you all of this, even though it is only with my eyes, do you still hurry to snatch up your hat and coat, as if, above all things else, you must be leaving? Why must you discard me now, when I am about to leave you in a short while anyway? Is there then no leeway? Will it always be that way?

Father, I keep on saying to myself,
I deserve to be forgiven.
I am not that bad child any more,
harbouring such secrets.
I have grown now.
I am old enough to take care of you.
I am old enough to understand you,
and all that you did for me,
and to understand how little it was that I appreciated
your goings out and your comings in.

I am no longer standing here, sheepish,
at your study door,
and you are no longer slowly turning to face me
in your creaking chair,
and then asking me what it is that I want,
and when you ask me like that, I forget of course.
I feel embarrassed. It is simply not enough to be saying
that most of all I am standing here now
because I want to see you seated in your customary chair
with the sunlight bathing your left hand,
and I want to have you watching me steadily
with that kindly look on your face,
not again about to chastise me at all
because I know now that I do not deserve it.

Is it the middle of winter here?
It is the middle of winter, surely,
because there is snow on the ground
outside the window,
and I saw someone just now
hurrying through the snow,
carrying a bucket.

And yet in my head it is all fuss and bother,
and I can scarcely breathe from all the heat.
I keep turning and turning in my bed.
There is no way to be comfortable,
And when I call out to someone – to anyone –
they do not come
because they are too exasperated with me,
with all these demands that I am making,

and just when I give them all up for lost forever,
two of them arrive, a girl and a man,
with the sweetest of sweet smiles,
and they lift me up between them,
making me feel lighter than air.
It is as if they are rocking me in a cradle
for the sheer pleasure it gives me.

Freddy

Frederick is scowling at me again,
and now he has turned his back on me,
and he will not let me see.
He tells me that it is all too private,
that world of his,
and that I am not to be admitted
because I do not belong there.

The only way is to wait a little while
until he becomes very very thirsty,
and then – it will be soon enough –
he will be pawing at my arm
and pointing to his mouth,
and then up to the tap
which is just beyond his reach,

and, for minutes on end,
I will not be able to understand
anything that he is trying to tell me
until the tears start welling
and I give in to him
because he is still my little brother
and none of that can be changed,
ever.

Resignation

Someone said just then,
someone in the doorway, looking,
that it is time to go,
and so I have made myself ready.

I have my hat here, my scarf and my gloves,
ranged around me on this bed,
ready to put them on at a moment's notice,
and they will surely tell me when.

This is my all-purpose scarf
and so no matter what the weather,
it will be ready to play its part
very satisfactorily.

As for these gloves, I know
that I am a little bit ashamed of them
because the fingers of the left hand
need some attention,

which, it has to be said,
I have not yet given them,
so the wind whistles up as far as the wrist,
and that is not exactly a pleasant feeling.

But they are the only ones here,
and they will just have to do.
As mother used to say when things went wrong:
prepare yourself, darling, for a bit of resignation.

I do not know why.
And nor do you,
So I don't know why
you are going on bothering me.

I have done the best that I could.
I couldn't go any further
because of the weather.
It was very sensible to turn back and re-consider.

Sometimes you need to sit
in front of a warming fire,
and weigh up all the options.
No one could disagree with that one.

Not even you.
Though it does seem to me
that you are always trying.

It's sickening, being here as me,
stuck inside this silly, useless body.
How many times do I need to say it?
There is just no point to it all, not any more.

I have come this far.
Why would you want
to try to persuade me
to go any farther?

For your sake,
is that it then?
You will miss me.
Well, you will just have to look at

a photograph or two.
You took enough of them in your time –
whether or not I managed to be
a willing sitter. I somehow doubt it.

Does God know?

I do hope so.
I have always trusted him.
I do not believe that he will let me down
at this particular moment.

Nine years in all
that I was Parish Warden,
doing my all – no, my bit – for St Paul's.
It was good for both of us.

I learnt to talk to people.
Well, I needed to, didn't I?
I had to do some directing.
People so quickly go astray.

It is like helping blind people across the road.
You cannot not do it.
Surely it is what life is for.

My Lingering Gratitude

Were you standing here just now,
giving a gentle lift
to my elbow?
I'm sure that it was your touch.
No one else feels quite like that.

And then you went to speak to me.
You opened your mouth to say some words.
I had such an appetite for them.
It is almost as if I knew before you spoke
what you would be saying.

And yet you did not speak.
You closed your mouth, quite gently,
and then, just as gently, withdrew your hand.
I still turned to smile my thanks.
I still, even now, feel so happy, so grateful.

The Chair Beside the Door

You promised to come
the day after tomorrow.
You threw that promise out so quickly,
so carelessly almost,
I scarcely heard you say it.

And yet you did say it because
the moment I got back,
I wrote it down in large letters
on the kitchen calendar.
I knew that you would not disappoint me.

Which is why, when the day came,
I was so ready and waiting
on the chair beside the door.
It felt all the realer for the fact
that I was wearing my gloves, my hat
and my best outside coat.

How much have you always remembered me?
No one can tell, of course.
One moment in four perhaps,
that is how often I remember you,
though even that feels so rough and ready.
You know what I mean though –
and especially if you happen to be
remembering at this moment,
when the wind has just blown up,
and there is such a mood of vague,
though heady, expectation.

Philip

He was with me all too briefly,
at those tea parties
in Hampstead Garden Suburb,
smiling bashfully at my elbow,
and then he was lost to me,
or so I was told by the letter
from the ministry,
forwarded to me by his adoring mother.

I saw her much in the early days
after his departure.
I could see her in his eyes.
Had she ever laughed –
which she did not –
I might have heard him in her laughter.

Did she want me there? I am not sure.
There was little warmth between us,
on those late October days,
so much bitterer than usual.
We exchanged news from time to time
in the later years.
And then we lost touch with each other.

Frederick's Favourite Enemy

I am here to tell you all a story!
I said it in my best firm voice,
and then I clapped my hands to get some attention.
They were always so maddening.

Frederick was the worst, as usual.
He never even pretended to be listening.
I watched him drifting around at the back,
playing at aeroplanes,
with his arms rising and falling.

Frederick! I shouted at last.
I just couldn't stop myself.
My voice was trembling.
He raised his head very slowly.

It was as if the sound was coming to him from far away,
somewhere way beyond the English Channel,
where the enemy was always located.

I never know quite where I am any more, and that is the worst of it, that I no longer feel quite lucid. I try to tell them how much this bothers me, and although I am quite sure that I register the pain and the distress on my face, and although they in their turn look up into my face with such kindness and patience, and even take hold of my hand and rub it, quite vigorously too, I am no longer convinced that the words are the right ones, not exactly. In fact, I am convinced that they are the words that I do not really want to choose at all. They sound, even to me, like crude approximations, spillings from the mouth of a jabbering ghost somewhere near me. And what is the good of that? It is all perfectly useless and completely maddening. Words simply don't seem to be working for me as they once used to. You would never know now that I had once been a college graduate. I am quite glad that you don't have to see me as I am, though I feel sad to be saying it. You would scarcely recognise me.

Andrew Marvell – almost everything. To me he is inexhaustible. Thomas Hardy for his elegies to his dead wife. Eliot's *Four Quartets*, of course, because, in part, they bring back the war years. They were a sort of bulwark, I always felt, against the general universal barbarity, the imminent collapse of civilisation as we knew it – which, thank god, never happened. Perhaps poetry did help just a little, in so far as it was always such an inward consolation, and has remained so, of course. I need it as much as I need food and drink, I have always thought, even though my own efforts as a versifier have been most feeble. None of my books are with me here. Where are my books now? Have I lost them?

All afternoon we seemed to be drifting towards the coast, and Edith, of course, was standing at the very front of the boat with a sort of crude plastic megaphone, booming out just the one word over and over again: Oxford, Oxford, Oxford. She needs that word like people in distress at sea need a life jacket. Then, a little later, I was standing on a very steep and windy slope, with the sun blinding my eyes, feeding a nubby piece of very hard bread to a lovely goat which lived in an unusually small pound in the Albanian village where we were staying, and Edith was talking to us about the fact that we would be crossing back to Crete very, very early in the morning, so we would need to get some sleep. I don't know why Edith has to be so bossy. Perhaps it is because she is the leader of the group. Because she always knows everything, no one else is granted any space whatsoever even to know the teeniest little bit. Needless to say, everyone finds it completely exasperating, and no one ever tries to stop it happening either. So it is a little bit miserable here from time to time. At other times, of course, it is perfectly lovely. We all know just how hard she has worked to please us. Life – even when you are striving to live a good life – can be such a muddle.

Every part of the day resembles every other part of the day. There is no way of differentiating one thing from another any more. And worse still, I no longer have the will or the energy to do anything about it. I am just too weak now. All I am capable of doing is looking out through my eyes. I feel so helpless, so worthless. Even my hand is too heavy to be lifted.

We were running, tearing through the gorse, going faster and faster, all five of us, waving and shrieking. The grown ups were calling to us from behind, but as we ran and ran, gaining speed, their voices became fainter, ever fainter. Douglas was in the lead. He was egging us on to run faster still down the path towards the beach, slapping at his side as he ran as if he was a jockey whipping a horse along the flat. We could see it spread out beneath us down there, flung out like a huge handkerchief, the beach, with a long lip of grey sea at the edge of the sand, where the cove opened out. I felt as if I was gulping in more and more air. I was beginning to get dizzy with the excitement of it all. It felt as if my head was filling up with air, inflating like a huge balloon – a Zeppelin or something – and soon I would rise up off the ground, rise, up and up, into the air. And then my foot hit, caught on, something, and I stumbled and fell, and I remember nothing after that. Everything went black – just like at the cinema, before it begins to happen.

Philip, are you there for me? I do believe that I saw you just now, and you were wearing – oh miracle! – your best demob suit, and I was admiring the look of you in it, how slim you still were, lean as a whippet, and thinking to myself: thank god that it is all now over, and that we can breathe again, and walk in the open air, and see the lights on in the shops out in the winter street, and even, perhaps on a Thursday, take ourselves off to the cinema, clutching a small bag of sweets to share. Wouldn't that be just heavenly, Philip?

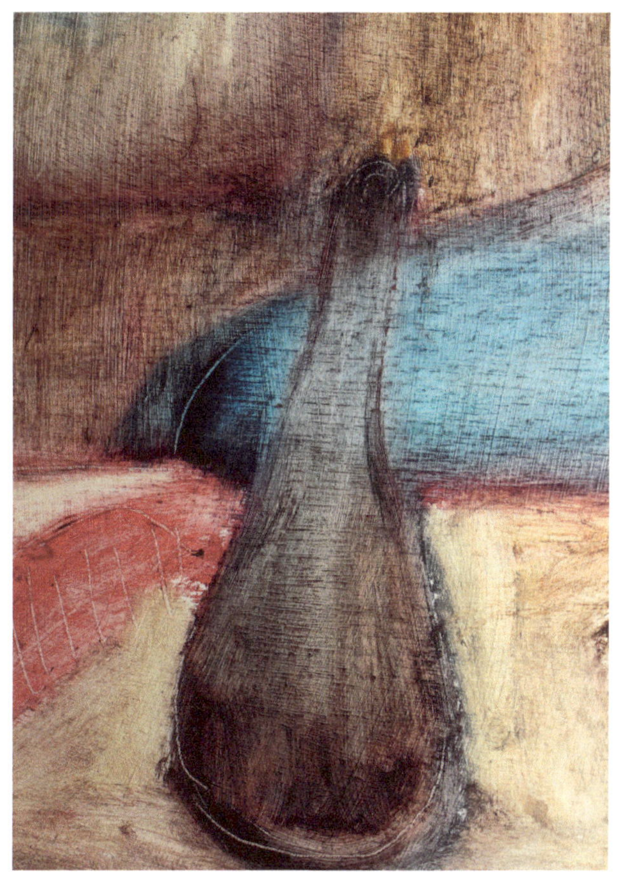

My two sisters are both so dear to me. Maggie is so loud, and June quite the opposite. How could they have been made so differently? And do I love them equally? Maggie angers and bothers me so much, but when she sets off crying again, I run to her immediately, and enfold her with my arms, tight-squeezing, until the sobbings die away. She always wipes her tears on my sleeve at the end in a matter of fact sort of way, as if I am a towel. And then, quite brusquely, she walks away and, soon enough, the noise strikes up again. There is always such a general hullabaloo around her, as if it is in her nature to set the world in a ferment. June is so different. She shares so little. I always feel that she lives a secret life, located somewhere deep inside her, and that to be there, in that tiny little dark space, is what she enjoys most of all. Being out in the world is of secondary importance. As are the people who happen to inhabit that world. When I walk towards her, she tends to gently close the book that she is reading – she is always reading something or other – in order to prevent me seeing the words that she was just now reading. Or perhaps that is not true at all. Perhaps, when she sees me approaching, she feels the need to give me some attention. She does not want to be seen to be snubbing me. Yes, perhaps that's what it is, a surfeit of kindness.

Is it an October day out there? Is that why so many leaves have fallen? I wish that someone would go out there, and tidy them away into manageable heaps, so that the world could look a little less untidy. I shall do it myself, in my blue boiler suit. I shall open the door of the garden shed directly beneath the kitchen window, and I shall seize hold of the rake, and I shall march out there in order to be a lesson to all of them. And I shall do that after I have just taken this pill that I am being offered – and the nurse agrees with me that that is what I must do, in that order of priorities, to take this pill, and then have a little sleep in order to gather all the strength that I will need for the raking of all those horse chestnut leaves, which are making the lawn look so untidy. And she says – says! – that she will come out to help me the moment that her shift is over. You say that, I tease her, and she smiles at me because she knows that I am on to something. It is pink and oval in shape, and it sits on my hand, in the centre of the palm of my hand, unstirring unless I gently shake it, like a very small pink oval baby. And it goes down so easily with a sip from this glass of water that she always holds out to me, the dear girl. She so much deserves a lovely husband. I always say that to her.

I have no wish to go back and re-live my life. I have had just as much as I deserved, and I have enjoyed it immensely. I always give thanks for that. And now it is time to go, so I want you to listen to me carefully. Do not regard it as at all odd or at all distasteful, what I am about to tell you. Everyone should behave in this way. It is the sensible thing to do. If you are the one to find me in my bed, lying perfectly still, please try not to upset yourself. What will have happened to me is completely natural, and exactly what I have always wanted for myself, to die peacefully in my own bed, in my own home. It would be no use at all to prolong my life unnecessarily, so that I could not get about any more on the bus or not shop for my vegetables at Berwick Street Market. That would be hateful. So, quietly, when you see that I am no longer stirring, lift up the receiver of the telephone in the hall, and arrange for my body to be taken away. I don't want any fuss of any kind. I know that you will be sad, but what you must tell yourself is that all this is exactly as it should be, and, moreover, that it is what I wanted. And thank you for doing this for me.

I organise the games for them, around the kitchen table, on a Wednesday morning, and they are always so grateful to be here together, leaning over the dominoes or shuffling the cards. Some of them barely get out at all, and it is quite an effort even to climb the steps to the house, and they do it because they love coming here. It requires almost no effort on my part whatsoever. I am happy to give them something, to remove them for a brief time at least, from their lonely rooms, and have them here, seated in a circle, on one or another of my hotchpotch of chairs, even occasionally saying a few words to each other. Because that is often one of the consequences of living on your own, you forget the art of talking, the art of human communication. Well, that is true of most people. There are one or two who never stop talking, and one is often quite relieved to see the back of them.

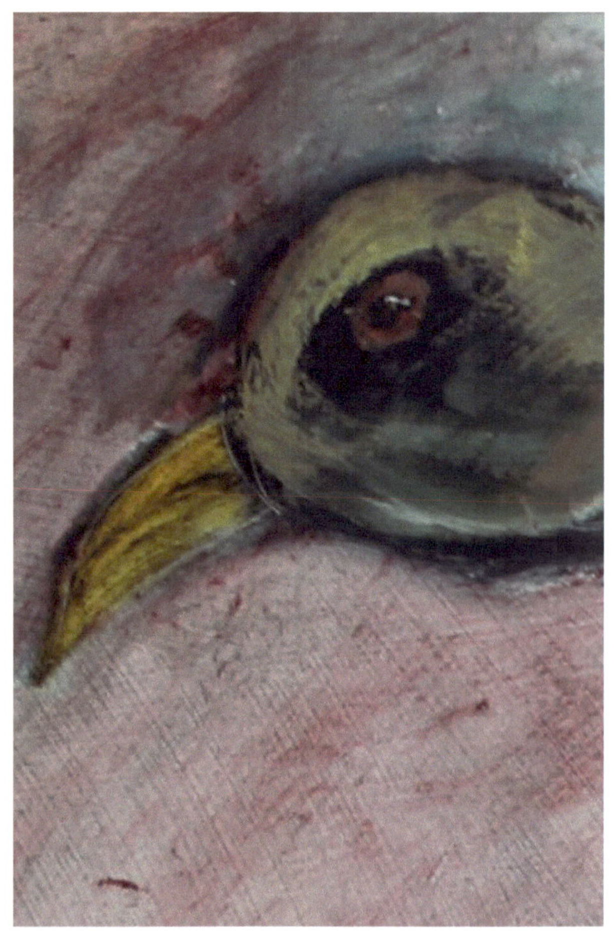

I am always very particular about vegetables. Sometimes the stall holders do not like the way in which I test them for their firmness, but because I am now an old lady – very, very old to the youngest, who look at me with some shock as if by rights I ought to be dead already – I manage to get away with a great deal. Worst of all are those rude people who try to push in front of me just as the bus is drawing up to the kerb. I manage to swing my reticule at their lower leg – the tender bit of the calf, just below the knee – without actually ever looking in their direction, and when they lean down to rub it, and give me a filthy look, I smile back at them as if I am living the life of a dreamy old thing who is not quite in control of her own shopping basket, and does not have an ounce of malice in her body. They never say anything of course – and nor do I, needless to say – because they would be unlikely to confess to their rudeness, would they? Through their fury they forgive me for being so old and so careless.

Sometimes it is quite an effort to climb the steps up Matrimony Way, past the church, and back into Rectory Grove. Perhaps I ought to buy less. On the other hand, I hate making unnecessary journeys. I always think that once a week should suffice for the necessaries. What always pleases me of course is the sight of mother in the window, waving, gently waving. She is like a fond old dog, the way she sits at the window, looking out for me, waiting for my return to the dear house. That is what I always call it. When something goes wrong or she complains about a little leak in the roof or something, I always say to her: let the dear house be. It can't help it, you know. We are all inclined to get a bit leaky as we age. Let Marion upstairs see to it. Let her put a bucket underneath the drips as she always does. We have quite enough to think about with the ground floor and the basement. She always enjoys my little pleasantries about the house. They mollify her. They soothe her. Sometimes she even touches the wall behind the *chaise longue* in the window after I have just said something, and then mutters: it *is* such a dear place. No wonder it has its aches and pains like the rest of us. Then I settle her red rug over her, and she may even sleep for a little while.

Death, I always think, is a marvellous thing. Provided, of course, that you are ready for it. You must be ready. Most people are not, and especially not the old people. You can see such fear in their eyes, fear of decrepitude, fear of loneliness, fear of what may happen next. Perhaps it is I who am the lucky one, in not fearing it. It is just a matter of passing from one state to another. You see, I know that I shall be welcome where I am going. I know that Brian and Desmond and Dove will all be waiting for me, so that we can continue our conversations. There will be so much to talk about, and it will be easier then because there will not be so many distractions. There will not be the usual hullabaloo. It is often quite difficult to talk to them when one is alive and busy because there are so many other people to attend to; as a Parish Warden one has so many obligations. Then it will all be quite different. We will be at rest then, at peace with one another. All the irritants will have taken themselves off elsewhere.

Maggie told me that she was going to paint a petal from the creeper rose next to the window. I told her not to pull it off or mother would be angry. She looked a bit sheepish when I said that. I noticed that her left hand was tucked away behind her back. Show me, I said, quite quietly at first. She did one of her small, angry pouts, staring down at the rug, which she was scuffing with her toe end. Show me what you have in your hand, Maggie, I said, pointing. Very slowly, very reluctantly, she drew her closed fist out from behind her back, and held it out in front of me, turned down. It was bunched. The knuckles were an angry red. Now open it. Please. She twisted it the right way up, very slowly, and did as I asked. There it was, the crumpled petal. I breathed a very heavy sigh of disapproval. If you don't tell on me, I'l give you my Saturday penny, she said, defiantly. She never apologises for anything. I don't know how she came to be a member of this family. She is so unlike the rest of us. Perhaps she was a terrible mistake.

The month of July was always prettiness everywhere. And so carefree too. We used to walk out together, hand in hand, Maggie and June and Freddy and I, in a long line, so pleased to belong to each other, thinking about the fact that it was summer and holidays, and that the days were so long you hardly ever slept because it was always so exciting to have so much light in the sky, even into the late, late hours of night, which were usually, at other times of year, the bedtime hours or else. In July, nobody even thought about the fact that there would be winter again. And then there would be the exciting thought, bright as a light bulb in our heads, that we would all be going somewhere soon, the whole family as one, without school exercise books or spelling tests, that we would sit on a beach together, probably in Cornwall, and just talk and throw balls and let our toes grip the sand, picking up little amounts of sand between our scrunched toes, and see who could carry them farthest without spilling too much, silly things like that.

And it didn't really matter what you did – within reason – because you could do anything, and at any time of day – within reason. And nobody ate at tables. You ate sandwiches on your knee in front of the sea, trying to make sure that the sand didn't get in to them because then they would get spoiled – or, most likely, Maggie's would get spoiled because she was always just so careless, and then, maddeningly, there would be much much less for everyone else because mother would shout out: family sharing! And there was nothing we could do about it when that happened except to glare at Maggie for ages after until she said or did something really comical with her face, which made you love her all over again, even though she *definitely* didn't deserve it.

I even thought that I would talk to her because I could see that she was so much worse off than me. No one ever came to see her. No one ever addressed her by her name, which was Audrey. I had heard the nurses say it to each other, but never to her though because she never looked anywhere except at the ceiling, and she certainly never spoke. And so I rose up on my elbow, looked across at her face in profile, propped up on the pillow completely motionless, and then I said her name. Did she speak back to me? No, she did not. She was too far beyond all that, I could recognise that fact. All the same, I wanted some part of her to know that someone nearby was thinking about her, so I said her name again, and saying it aloud made me reflect upon the fact that it was a pretty name, and that when she was young she must have felt pleased to hear it spoken out loud. She must have felt pleased to be called to: Audrey. *Audrey, darling, come in for tea...* And then I do believe that something did happen, not much, but something all the same, something worth remarking upon. I thought that I saw her eyebrow rise, slightly quizzically. Perhaps some part of her brain or her heart or her soul had been able to recognise that someone was calling out to her. It gave me such pleasure to see it.

The Boy on the Step

Were you there when I opened the door to you?
There was this strange, awkward boy on the step,
with dusters and other household things
organised on a little tray,
and I could not say no to him
because he showed me his card
speaking of polite officialdom,
and I felt so sorry for him and his thin, cold hands,
but the fact is that it was you I was expecting
when the doorbell rang,
and the look on his face seemed to suggest
that he might know of your coming too,
which explains why, when you didn't come
for hours and hours after he had gone,
I truly felt so woebegone.

Yes, and since you ask,
I have always had more than enough
to make me happy.
How much money does a single woman
who pleases herself ever really need?
I have my television for the evening
when I am a little too tired to read my poetry
because poetry does demand attention.
It is not something one skates over
like the evening newspaper.
I have food in the refrigerator.
I have my grass seed to cover up
the bald patches in the garden.
That is where I spend my time
on a Sunday afternoon,
after morning service, before and after lunch.
I put on my boots in rainy weather
and I do a little good honest digging.
There is something fine about dealing with
clay on the boots.

Father, if you are there now, I do want you to know that I did the best that I could with a good deal of rather unpromising material, by which I am referring to my own life. Not that I am ungrateful for what you vouchsafed me, nothing like that. It was my duty to make of it what I could. Isn't that the meaning of Free Will, that you hand all this down to us like a marvellously unexpected gift, and that it is then up to us to shape it as we are able? Some do better than others. A number are absolute marvels, amongst whom I would not count myself. I was always a rather small thing, in stature and – how should I put it? – intellectual and emotional reach. I did what I could with my meagre talents. The older I grew, the more I found myself capable of reaching out to people, to give back to them at least a little of what I had received from you. I had never expected much from other people until then, and it was at that point that I began to discover that I had not expected to receive much back because I had never had the capacity to give much out. I had always been too narrow and too costive – a little like an old horse with blinkers. And then my duties at the church came to my rescue. I went out beyond the accepted limits of myself. At first it was if I was being pushed out in a small boat towards turbulent seas. I was obliged to speak in a voice of welcome to those I found unattractive in all sorts of different ways. Some were boorish and loud-mouthed. Others were quite nauseatingly self-satisfied. I had to approach them all as if they were the children of God. I had to offer them the hand of friendship. It was so difficult at first. I could scarcely recognise my own speaking voice or the words that I was using. Surely I was playing the hypocrite by showing them such kindness, a kindness that I scarcely felt. Then, little by little, as they warmed to me and reached out to me in my turn, I began to see that the welcoming had become a two-way process. As a result of my approaches, they were softening as human beings, and welcoming me into their lives too, and it was nourishing for me to respond in my turn.

There is so little to be seen here,
so little for the eye to be enriched by.
My own impotence of gaze consumes me,
my own impotence of body.

Just now, that fly on the wrong side of the window,
to be looking in, to be gone again.
I followed its movements for a little while,
and then, as ever, I wearied of the commitment.

A hand lying still on a sheet, my hand,
shrivelled thin, pinky blue in colour.
An effort to describe the same,
an effort to give it the attention it scarcely deserves.

What would you ask of me now?
It is all perfectly useless, you know.
I am fit for nothing at all.
I am lying helpless as an empty sack.

Where would you take me now?
Nothing would please me, you know.
The young are all eager to be gone.
I too – though in a rather different way.

Who did you say that you were?
I knew you just then. Not now.
You have newly fragmented in front of me.
I wish there were laughter somewhere.

My father, be kind to the dead.
They are so incapable.
Darkness is as much as they know.
Perhaps they will come to see far.

There are angel voices out in the corridor.
Or perhaps I am mistaken.
Perhaps such sweet sounds were an illusion.

There are heavenly footsteps approaching.
No, it is the nurse's shoes again.
She is looking in to reassure me.

My body is being lifted.
I feel a great releasing.
They tell me it is bath time.

Out There or In Here

Out there, yes, where the light falls aslant.
I know now that it is out there in the corridor
    that everything happens.
I heard a gentle singing voice once – and even a trickle of laughter.
There is not the same solemnity
or the same morbid rigidity out there.
I am sorry, but nothing of any consequence happens in here.
I myself am not a happening of any kind, not any more.

Out there though there are many general whisperings going on,
and I wish that I were a part of it, though not truly.
It is quite enough to be in here, in my bed,
alone with my own company.
I am as contented as I need to be
because I know that there is to be no sharing any more.
I no longer have the energy to share.
It is a matter of the slow consolidation of
the dwindling little that there is.
I am circling, very slowly, around my own fading memories.

I do still love the light though,
the way it creeps in
to interrupt and then confound the darkness.
I have always been afraid of the dark.
I have always prayed that the long hours of darkness
might be dispelled
and that light might return to console me.
And so it does and has done, repeatedly.

Take my mittened hand again, father,
because we are now very close to where the traffic comes,
and I am not to be trusted to walk across this road on my own.

You have told me that I must not walk on my own until I am old,
and now I am older than you,
and I cannot be trusted to walk on my own

without the help of your reassuring hand
because the confidence I once had I now seem to have lost.
I need your guidance once again, beloved father.

Do not leave me here on my own before I need you.
Do not tell me that you have already gone.
Do not weary me again with words of exasperation.

My Requests

I have asked for the sheets to be laundered and folded.
I have asked for the mattress to be fumigated.
I have asked for the bed to be pushed back flush with the wall
so that it is no longer any bother to knees and legs.

I have asked for the windows to be flung open wide,
and for the curtains to be laundered to perfection.
I have asked for the air to come whistling around me
and for a certain dazzle to be present.

I am standing here cleanly on my legs,
wholly unencumbered by night things, all that frippery,
waiting patiently to be gathered up,
new spun as any child of heaven.

Mother came to the front door to greet me. She took one of the lighter shopping bags from my hand, which I did not want her to do because, as I have repeatedly warned her, I am the shopper now, mother, and you must be very careful not to harm yourself with the least little exertion. And yet she cannot bear to see me doing all the carrying. She simply will not listen, so I have to work myself up into a semblance of crossness, and she has to pretend to be upset by my words and, head bowed, without saying a single word, retreat to the *chaise longue* in the window, with me frowning after her as if she is a small pet to be chastened. Rather like Elizabeth's chihuahua, that silly little nothing of a dog.

Let me return there in all my nakedness (should I say purity?). Let me return to the place of origins. Let me return to the place of renewal. Let me return to the place where everything must have an ending.

The light buffets, slaps, makes its intolerable incursions. It has not always been so. This is why you must remonstrate with me, on this day of days, before the window makes its exaggerated claims. Clarity! Truthfulness! A life beyond all other lives!

I lie here on my back, as still as I am able. Eyes firmly closed, I see myself walking away from this place, from this place of ending, back to where I have always lived. My stride is firm, purposeful. I am pouting a little, as I so often do. I am facing into the wind, facing down the wind. My reticule is swinging at my side. Friends, old and new, greet me from time to time.They point the way back to my cherished places. I am a Clapham woman, of sixty years long standing.

So much of this is no longer quite true. It has been my choice. I have chosen the final embrace of death over the burden of too long a life. And so they have brought me here.They have transported me here of my own volition. I have made my pact with them. My arms are pinioned to my sides so that they do not go astray. I have been reduced to the condition of a helpless child. And yet I lie here contented enough. I would not have it otherwise.

Life's portion now is a meagre one. I eat so little. I see so little. My words are so sparing few.

I am touched by the way that death, my oncoming death, is already touching me, so lightly, as if with its finger tips. I would summon them up, all of them, if I could, but there would always be too many. I simply would not have sufficient space for them all. I must be choosy. I must be finicky. I must pluck them out, one by one, like fruits from a stall in Berwick Street Market or like words from a dictionary.Words have always been so dear to me.There is so much of death in me. I am sated with the onset of death. It is almost too rich, too sweet a syrup. Part of myself would wish to put it away.

There is the onset of death everywhere hereabouts. These rooms, these corridors know nothing else. Death is the most regular and most dependable of visitors. It is why we must cherish the ever dwindling smallness of ourselves.

There is precious little walking.
There is very little firmness of step.
Footfalls are light, almost breath-like.
They come. They go. They start. They end.

Am I resigned now to losing the world? Am I resigned to losing myself? Which would I fear or dislike the more? Neither the one nor the other. I have already divested myself of what I regard as the rich, fleeting unreality, of self and of world.

The light is burning, and it is not yet dawn. The bells are ringing, and there is no church to be seen. These are my twin consolations: light and that careless, carefree carillon of bells. I am able to summon them, now, such glorious things as these, as if at whim, from everywhere. It is such a gift.

Here is the first of my childish days, I have drawn it with the aid of a crayon, such is the appeal of its brightness. And now I repeat it in so many words.

I look up from my reading. It is a Saturday morning again, and the house is empty. I am at a loss to know where my footsteps are taking me. The door to the street is open. Your note has blown away again. I am not running to catch it. The poem itself is fragmentary. It is the work of a moody child, a child eager to snatch favours, verbal favours, from the air. The air itself hereabouts is a thing of beauty, free-floating in all directions. Only the others alarm me just a little, the way they pronounce upon me.

I am at a loss to know
Where you might now be placing me.
Lives come and go.
My life comes and goes.
It is all such a strange, sidereal drifting.
How much is there still to be read?
I have dozed. I have dreamed.
I have left this room in a hurry,
Shaking the dust from my feet.

I am sick again, unto death.
Nothing helps me
But the wind's soughing.
It carries me up into its arms
From where I can see the landscape
Spreading out before me.

No one is there, blocking my path.
No one has stepped up to chastise me.
No one has spoken of my obligations.
Who is looking at what?
It is the path itself which is disappearing
To left or to right of me.
There are no faint echoings.

Was that your hat I saw just then
From the fence post hanging?
This level of self-regard is killing me.
When I spoke to you of all of this,
You roundly rebuffed me.
You have no mission to be here, you said.

So much love lost
Or vanished in a single cry –
Yesterday's.
Did you not ask then
For this to happen?
Were your tears then spontaneous,
As if you might have been thinking
Of someone else?
I do not believe any of this.
You must be lying to yourself.
Silence is slipping its threads between,
Thinking all the while:
You must surely understand.

I have explained all this to myself,
The way the day has blown in
Like an old man tired of so much walking,
Sitting down now, out of the sun,
And no one even there to be noticing.

Long before the earth
Had grown accustomed to
The idea of my birth,
This stone had taken
Its vow of silence.

My friend, take this for a warning.
You will not be as you have always been.
The houses will disappear from view.
There will be a great scraping back to nothing.

I am standing as a child on the library steps,
Books in hand, as always,
Re-telling over to myself
The stories that I have just read.

I am standing as a child on the library steps,
Books in hand, as always.
Then they called me forward to the desk,
Where I presented myself
In the guise of an eager child,
Sweat-soaked, over-burdened.

Start it here.Why not?
It will unfold in the telling.
There is nothing more to be done or said.

None of them seemed quite as vivid to me
As the life I was living in the park at my back,
With its fountain playing,.

I looked down.
I caught myself admiring
The sheen of my knuckles.

All told, there is nothing for me here
Except this exaggerated acknowledgement
Of a window, a door.
And then perhaps a breath of wind
Through that window, that door,
Fleeting and intermittent.

Shortness of breath.
The beginnings of a fever.
Nothing of much consequence any more.
And then when the sun makes its faint affirmations,
Noon or thereabouts,
On this day or some other,
We will surely be together again,
Hoping for the impossible to happen.

On these library steps,
We are on the threshold of all knowledge.
I lie to myself, of course.
There is nothing to be known.

My dear dead child,
I have never known you.
You never reached out,
Opening your arms to me.
And I, I never spoke mother words back to you.
We owe each other an apology.

I take charge of my own back garden. It is my cherished plot, set apart from the world's prying eyes. It is all mine to take charge of. I patrol it. I tend to it, pacing up and back the narrow concrete path in my green wellington boots. I am also wearing my old boiler suit, the blue one, and with the aid of the secateurs, which I hold in my hand, I reach, reach up to heights near impossible to one so short as me, busying myself with the task of pruning the leaves which part conceal the Passion Flowers I must see from my kitchen window.

When I go to look out of my kitchen window, leaning over the gas stove, snapping the lighter into the hiss of gas emitted from the front burner, it is at such times as these that I embrace with my eye the glory of my Passion Flowers, out there, in the stirring air, climbing the trellis, as if they didn't have a care in the world. I sometimes think that I live for those flowers.What would I do if one of them were to be violated without my permission?

I have never wanted to leave you.
I have never wanted to say goodbye.
What exactly does all this mean though?
The fact is that I never wanted to be as close to you
As you always were in those letters we exchanged,
So often, and with such excitement.

It was in those letters that I knew you most of all,
When we came so breathing close to each other.
We were in love then, weren't we?
And later, when we met at a bus station in Swansea,
Or on the threshold of a bedroom in a small hotel,
When all was slightly grey and flustered and coming on wintery,
It was never quite the same now, was it?

As long as my eye roams around this room, no matter how little my head may be stirring, I can truthfully tell myself that I am not yet dead, and this does not entirely please me.They bother me, the ones who come to call, the ones who lift me and shift me from side to side, often so distractedly – I hear them whispering to each other.The woman with the crucifix pendant is the worst of all. She fixes my eye with such a pitiful look of sentimental piety that I would throw water into her face had I the strength to do so. I would drown her in water, with perfect contentment. I would hold her head down, down, with such a fierceness of grip, until she has ceased to twitch. And then I would lean back, sigh, and give thanks.

Maggie

Maggie, even though we have had
our many differences, major and minor,
I do so want you to come
and sit down here beside me –
See, I have patted the bed's edge
to indicate exactly where –
so that we can remember our days together.

Maggie, we have not spoken for a long, long while,
and I do not know exactly why that should be.
Did we drift away from each other?
Or did you, on some day that I have now forgotten (sad to say),
simply die on me?

I do remember how, as a child, you were very very sickly,
and we were all terribly concerned about you.
So many nights you were up so late, inhaling the Friar's Balsam
through that terrible hacking cough of yours.
It always sounded so deep and so hollow
when echoing around the mixing bowl.

None of us could get to sleep.
We were all so concerned about you.
And then when you did go back to school
after goodness knows how many weeks,
we formed a line in your honour at the garden gate
just as if you were a war hero or something very similar.

Maggie, although we shouted at each other a lot
until we made each other hoarse with all the effort,
I do want you to know just how much I loved you
and still love you
even though you were always so maddening to me,
contradicting me at every end and turn,
stealing my best crayons,
and even pulling my hair out by the roots.

I forgive you for all that now.
All that I would ask is that you come here
and make yourself comfortable beside me
without tipping me out
because of your great weight these days.

You have not paid me a visit
for as long as I can remember,
and the trees outside are telling me,
with such insistence,
that it is already a very cold snap
of a day in December.

Not Making Amends

I cannot make amends
for all the wrong things I have done.
It would be quite impossible.
There are far too many of them,
and most are now forgotten.
The ones which are not stick up in the air
like a terrible throbbing finger
that it is quite impossible for any child
such as I was then to shake off.

I do not know what to do about it.
Saying sorry sounds so terribly lame,
and especially when there is no person
present to forgive you in your turn –
or perhaps they would rather not.
There is no one here to say except God.
Some nastinesses are perhaps
too terrible to be forgiven.
They are wounds which can never heal.
They stare back at you through your waking dreams
on odd days like today.

The Platelets Situation

Let me be perfectly clear.
I have no intention of staying here
for longer than is absolutely necessary.
I know that I am here for a very good reason.
The fact is that I can never get enough blood transfusions.
All may change for the better in God's good time,
though I do accept that it may not.

Be that as it may, I do need to see to the garden
because no one else will do it
as it requires to be done.
I am not sure that you quite understand
even though you are nodding your head in agreement.
You see, there is always so much tending –

which I do like, of course, but it is a long-term commitment
of which I would not wish to absolve myself.
The Japanese Knot Weed, for example,
must be kept in hand.
Are you the man for that sort of thing?
I myself rather doubt it, though you, I think, do not.

Being Thoroughly Tiresome

I am being a tiresome creature, I know that for a fact,
too demanding on occasions, and, at other times,
quite weak and needy and biddable – in fact, just like mother.

I do not see what there is to be done about it.
It is just as if these moods overtake me
like a strong wind blowing in from nowhere
when the hat gets clamped to the top of the head
and one can do nothing but live in hope.

I have always lived in hope, of course,
because that is what God demands of each of us.
I have done my best to be faithful.
I have stood the test, at least in part.
The race is always such a long one,
requiring such steadiness of routine –
like sweeping the stairs with a broom
again and again and again.
The fact is that it never seems to end until it ends.

Take Me Away

Dear God, take me away.
I know that I am ready.
There is really no good reason any more
to stay here in this world
where I have lived my life to the full and beyond.

I am such an encumbrance,
such a bother to so many, and that, as you are perfectly aware,
I have never wanted, not even for a single precious moment.

Could we not do it quickly and simply,
perhaps even this morning, for example,
when I have woken once again so early
to the knowledge of the perfect uselessness
of my continuing existence
here on this earth,
which I have loved so much,
and now for far too long.
Such is the nature of my special pleading.

Thinking

I was standing once on the corner,
facing the church,
prepared to walk down Matrimony Way
to take the bus into town,
as I have always done.

I had my bag in my hand
and my purse in the pocket
of my belted coat.
Things were as they had always been.
I caught myself thinking then:
What if, instead, I had married,
And was living now in Surrey
With a dog and two children?

I saw myself there, quite happy,
making brisk conversation with whomever,
and even smiling.
I would have done it, you know.
I would have risen to that different occasion.
I would have become that slightly different person
had the situation dictated,
had the war not spoken.
And then, feeling rather pleased by that outcome,
I made my way, and the sun was shining on me,
though the wind still blew up Iveley Road quite briskly.

Urgings

I know perfectly well that this kitchen is a little shabby,
But the fact is that I like it like this.
It is what I am accustomed to,
and I do not think that a central heating boiler
and radiators spread across the walls
would be much good to me at all.
What is the use of instant heat
When you can rub your hands together
to restore perfect circulation almost immediately?
Is this not what God expected us to do?
Why bring in new-fangled notions
When I live here perfectly happily
Around this kitchen table
With a perfectly good solid-fuel boiler at my back?
I would not want such changes as you are urging upon me.
I am quite happy being here as I am, and as I have always been.
I am one hundred per cent contented.
Please do remember that
when you feel inclined to persuade me
with the sweetest of words,
and for the purest of motives, I have no doubt,
to do things slightly differently.
The times have not changed
to quite the extent that you may believe,
my dear niece, my dear nephew.

The Interrupted Jigsaw Puzzle

It was not quite what I wanted.
I wanted to stay indoors at the kitchen table
as I always tend to do on a Thursday afternoon,
and finish the puzzle
that has been sitting on the tray half-done
since a week last Tuesday.

I would have picked up the pieces one by one
and then carefully considered,
drumming my lip with my thumb,
the shapes of the gaps,
and when I found one that seemed to correspond to
the shape in my hand, I would have laid it down.

There were only two or three still left to be done.
And now I may never finish it.
Do you quite understand
How much that means to me?

I want to be left to do it all on my own.
I am still perfectly capable, you know.
Sometimes I need to rest a little these days.
Today, for example, I had to sit
On this wall in Netherford Road
for as long as it took me to gather my strength,
and I simply did not know
that I had blacked out and slid to the ground.
They found me there quite soon,
and when I opened my eyes to you later,
I could see that you were a little angry with me.
I do not deny that it happened,
and that it caused you some anguish
for a while.
I will need to get out again though
when I feel I am ready.
I have always pleased myself,
and I have no intention of stopping now,
even though I am a little infirm.
This is how it must be.
I am not an awkward elderly lady.
That is not at all how I see it.
This is my favourite street of all.
I have lived here for as long as I can remember,
and there is nothing I would change
about my being here, nothing at all.

Vintage & Contemporary: Michael Glover and Ruth Dupré

Poet and art critic Michael Glover grew up in a small terraced house in Fir Vale, Sheffield, Ruth Dupré in a twenty-room rectory at Landbeach near Cambridge. Michael's books include eight collections of poetry, books of memoirs, and writings on art. He is art critic of the *Independent*. Ruth is a multi-media artist. She first worked as a ceramicist, and later became a painter, a hot-glass sculptor, a film-maker, and then a deft manipulator of fabric. Her work has been exhibited in group and solo shows throughout the world. In 2010 she won the Jack Goldhill Prize for Sculpture at the Royal Academy Summer Exhibition. They have two children, and they live together in Clapham, South London, in the same house that Aunt Honor Dupré, whose long and benign presence in their lives brought this book into being, bought in 1963 for £6000. This is their first collaborative work.

www.ingramcontent.com/pod-product-compliance
Lightning Source LLC
Chambersburg PA
CBHW041129100726
47911CB00002B/82

* 9 7 8 0 9 9 3 5 7 6 2 8 7 *